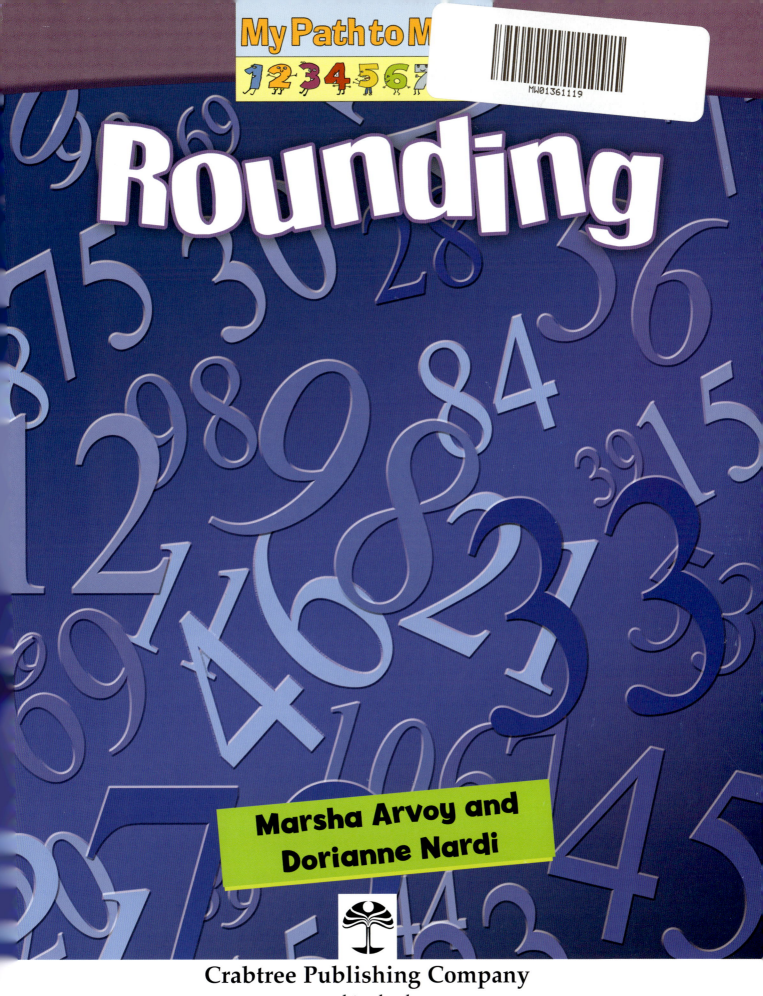

Author: Marsha Arvoy and Dorianne Nardi
Publishing plan research and development:
  Sean Charlebois, Reagan Miller
  Crabtree Publishing Company
Editor: Reagan Miller
Proofreader: Crystal Sikkens
Editorial director: Kathy Middleton
Project coordinator: Margaret Salter
Prepress technician: Margaret Salter
Coordinating editor: Chester Fisher
Series editor: Jessica Cohn
Project manager: Kumar Kunal (Q2AMEDIA)
Art direction: Cheena Yadav (Q2AMEDIA)
Cover design: Jasmeen Kaur (Q2AMEDIA)
Design: Ravinder Chauhan and Isha Khanna (Q2AMEDIA)
Photo research: Anubhav Singhal and Debabrata Sen (Q2AMEDIA)

Photographs:
Bigstockphoto: Maksym Dragunov: p. 19; Marko Beric : p. 21
Dreamstime: Sherry Sowell: p. 9 (top)
Istockphoto: Nicole S. Young: p. 5 (right child); Connie T. Ballash:
  p. 13; Don Nichols: p. 19
Photolibrary: Doug Menuez: p. 5 (except right child), 7 (top)
Shutterstock: cover, p. 15; Picsfive: p. 7 (bottom); Bruce Shippee:
  p. 9 (bottom); Tottles: p. 10, 11; Tereza Dvorak: p. 11; Danny E.
  Hooks: p. 13; Vakhrushev Pavel: p. 13; Sergey Shandin: p. 17;
  Alexander Motrenko: p. 19; Ryasick Photography: p. 19;
  Picsfive: p. 23

Library and Archives Canada Cataloguing in Publication

Arvoy, Marsha
    Rounding / Marsha Arvoy and Dorianne Nardi.

(My path to math)
Includes index.
ISBN 978-0-7787-6786-2 (bound).--ISBN 978-0-7787-6795-4 (pbk.)

    1. Rounding (Numerical analysis)--Juvenile literature.
I. Nardi, Dorianne II. Title. III. Series: My path to math

QA297.65.A78 2010   j513   C2010-901011-6

Library of Congress Cataloging-in-Publication Data

Arvoy, Marsha.
  Rounding / Marsha Arvoy and Dorianne Nardi.
     p. cm. -- (My path to math)
  Includes index.
  ISBN 978-0-7787-6786-2 (reinforced lib. bdg. : alk. paper) --
  ISBN 978-0-7787-6795-4 (pbk. : alk. paper)
  1. Rounding (Numerical analysis)--Juvenile literature. I. Nardi, Dorianne.
II. Title. III. Series.

  QA297.65.A78 2011
  513--dc22

                                                              2010004531

Crabtree Publishing Company

www.crabtreebooks.com   1-800-387-7650

Printed in China/072010/AP20100226

Copyright © **2011 CRABTREE PUBLISHING COMPANY**. All rights reserved. No part of this publication may be reproduced, stored in a retrieval system or be transmitted in any form or by any means, electronic, mechanical, photocopying, recording, or otherwise, without the prior written permission of Crabtree Publishing Company.

Published in Canada
Crabtree Publishing
616 Welland Ave.
St. Catharines, ON
L2M 5V6

Published in the United States
Crabtree Publishing
PMB 59051
350 Fifth Avenue, 59th Floor
New York, New York 10118

Published in the United Kingdom
Crabtree Publishing
Maritime House
Basin Road North, Hove
BN41 1WR

Published in Australia
Crabtree Publishing
386 Mt. Alexander Rd.
Ascot Vale (Melbourne)
VIC 3032

Contents

The School Fair 4

Learning the Rounding Rule 6

Estimate the Tickets 8

Rounding Length 10

More Rounding 12

Nearest Hundred 14

Rounding Money 16

Money Earned 18

Books for the School Library 20

Glossary 22

Index 24

MY PATH TO MATH

The School Fair

It is time to set up the school fair. The children have to count many things to get ready.

Their teacher is Miss Anita. She tells them that they will **round** numbers when counting. She explains that when rounding numbers we often change them to the **nearest ten**. Rounding numbers makes it easier to solve number problems. Rounding does not give an exact answer, but an **exact** answer is not always needed. We round numbers up or down to make them easier to use.

The teacher shows them a number line. They see that 12 is closer to 10 than 20. They round 12 down to the nearest ten.

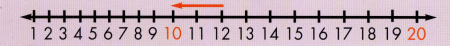

◀ A number line is a tool that can help with rounding.

Activity Box

Round the number 17 to the nearest ten. Use the number line to help you. Is 17 closer to 10 or closer to 20? Will you round down to 10 or up to 20?

Children will use rounding to help them set up for the fair.

MY PATH TO MATH

Learning the Rounding Rule

There are 38 children working at the fair. Miss Anita wants Allison to round 38 to the nearest ten.

Miss Anita gives Allison a rule for rounding numbers with two **digits**.

If the digit to the right is 1, 2, 3, or 4, round down to the lower 10. If the digit to the right is 5, 6, 7, 8, or 9, round up to the higher 10. Everything after the rounded number becomes a zero.

3**8** ← digit to the right

The number 38 can be rounded up to 40.

Activity Box

Ask a friend to write down a number between 10 and 20. Together, try to round the number to the nearest ten. Remember the rule!

This poem gives another way to think about rounding.

Find your number.
Look right next door.
Four or less, just ignore!
Five or greater,
add one more!

38 rounds up to 40

MY PATH TO MATH

Estimate the Tickets

There are 83 children coming to the fair. Each child needs a ticket. Miss Anita gives Allison and Lee the tickets left from last year's fair. She asks them to **estimate** how many tickets they have. Estimating will show if the number is close enough.

Allison counts 68 tickets. She rounds the number 68 to 70. Lee counts 36 tickets. He rounds the number 36 to 40. They **add** the rounded numbers together and get 110. They have enough tickets!

68 + 36 = 104
exact

70 + 40 = 110
rounded

◀ The rounded numbers are easier for Allison and Lee to add. The total is not exact, but it is a good estimate.

Activity Box

Round the numbers 28 and 13. Then add the numbers together. What is your answer? Now add 28 and 13 to get the exact number. Are the answers close? Which way was faster?

The children estimate the number of tickets by using rounding.

MY PATH TO MATH

Rounding Length

Allison gets the face-painting table ready. She must **measure** it to find a cloth that fits. She does not have a ruler, so she uses a **nonstandard tool** instead.

She uses tickets instead of inches or centimeters. She finds that the table is 22 tickets long.

Allison has a red cloth that is 20 tickets long. She has a blue cloth that is 30 tickets long. The red cloth is closer to the right size. Yet it is not long enough to cover the table. She uses the blue cloth instead.

Miss Anita explains that it is important to be **reasonable** when rounding numbers. It does not make sense to use a cloth that is too short.

The red cloth is ten tickets shorter than the blue one.

The blue cloth is 30 tickets long. The blue cloth will cover the entire table.

The 22 tickets show the length of the table.

The red cloth is 20 tickets long. The red cloth is too short.

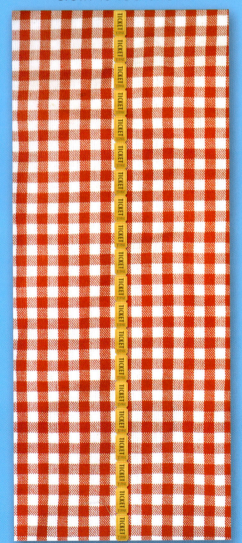

More Rounding

Miss Anita asks Lee to get the ring toss table ready. To play ring toss, people throw rings around bottles to win prizes. She tells him to set up 35 bottles.

Lee asks her how to round the number 35. The teacher reminds him of the rounding rule. When the digit to the right is 5, 6, 7, 8, or 9, round up to the higher 10.

Lee rounds 35 up to 40. Miss Anita tells him that this means he needs about 40 bottles. It is a good estimate. If they have 40 bottles, they will have extra if any bottles break.

Activity Box

Can you round the numbers 25 and 24? Round the numbers, and then add them together. Use the rounding rule you have learned.

Lee uses rounding to set up the ring toss game.

MY PATH TO MATH

Nearest Hundred

Miss Anita says that 328 prizes were given out at the fair last year. She asks Lee to round the number 328 to the **nearest hundred**.

To round to the nearest hundred, look at the digit to the right of the hundreds column. That digit is in the tens column. If that number is a 1, 2, 3, or 4, round down. If it is 5, 6, 7, 8, or 9, round up. Round down or up to the nearest hundred.

300	20	8	= 328
hundreds	tens	ones	

The number 2 is less than 5 so we round down to 300.

The number 328 rounded to the nearest hundred is 300. This means that 300 is a reasonable number of prizes to count out. After all, they will have extra prizes in the box!

Activity Box

If your school calendar has 182 days, would you round up to 200 or round down to 100? Explain your thinking.

How many prizes does Lee need? He can use a number line to round 328 to the nearest hundred.

MY PATH TO MATH

Rounding Money

Allison and Lee have $5.00 to spend for lunch. Miss Anita takes them to buy two slices of pizza. The slices cost $1.40 each. The **total** cost is $2.80. She asks them to round to the nearest dollar. That way, they will know about how much money will be left.

Miss Anita tells them to be careful when rounding numbers with **decimal points**. Look at the number to the right of the decimal point and follow the rounding rule.

$2.80 ◀ If the number is 1, 2, 3, or 4, round down. If it is 5, 6, 7, 8, or 9, round up.

Allison and Lee round $2.80 to $3.00. Next they **subtract** $3.00 from $5.00. They find they will have about $2.00 left.

Activity Box

If you had $3.00 and spent $1.90, about how much would be left? Round $1.90 to the nearest dollar. Subtract that number of dollars from $3.00. Would you have enough money to buy a snack that costs $1.00?

Would Allison and Lee have enough money to get a third slice?

MY PATH TO MATH

Money Earned

Allison and Lee count the money earned at each of their booths at the fair. Allison counts $32.37 from the face-painting booth. Lee counts $27.95 from the ring toss booth. They want to know about how much they earned in total.

Miss Anita tells them to round the numbers to the nearest dollar. She reminds them to look at the number to the right of the decimal point. Everything after the rounded number becomes a zero.

Allison $32.37 ⟶ $32.00
Lee $27.95 ⟶ $28.00

They add $32.00 and $28.00. They find out that they earned about $60.00!

Activity Box

You have 13 marbles, and your friend has 19 marbles. Round each number to the nearest ten. Then add them together. About how many marbles do you have in total?

Adding money is easier if you round the numbers.

MY PATH TO MATH

Books for the School Library

The fair raises $168 on Saturday and $123 on Sunday. Miss Anita asks the children to round the numbers to the nearest ten. Then she asks them to add the two numbers together to estimate the total.

Allison and Lee round $168 to $170. They round $123 to $120. They add the numbers together and get $290. That money will buy new books for the school library!

```
  170
 +120
 ————
  290
```

Activity Box

Rounding works in your life, too! Imagine going to the store. You buy milk for $3.80 and a loaf of bread for $1.12. About how much money do you need? Round the numbers to the nearest dollar. Then add them to get the total.

Imagine adding together the number of books on both shelves. You could use rounding to help you find the total.

MY PATH TO MATH

Glossary

add To combine two numbers

decimal points Dot symbols that separate numbers greater than 1 from numbers less than 1

digits Any of the numbers from 0 to 9

estimate To make a good guess based on things you know, or the guess itself

exact Precise or correct

measure To determine the size of an object

nearest hundred Closest hundred, such as 100, 200, 300, and so on

nearest ten Closest ten, such as 10, 20, 30, and so on

nonstandard tool An unusual object used to measure something; a measuring object that is not standard in the way that a ruler is standard

reasonable Makes sense

round Change digits in a number while keeping the value similar

subtract To take a part away from a whole

total The sum or whole amount

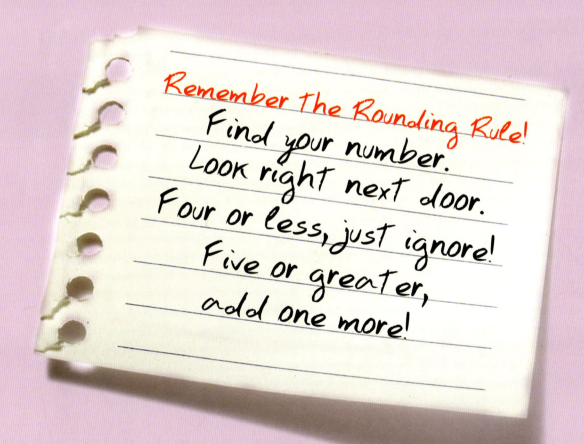

Index

add 8, 12, 18–21
decimal points 16, 18
digits 6, 14
estimate 8, 9, 12, 20
exact 4, 8
measure 10
nearest dollar 18, 20
nearest hundred 14–15
nearest ten 4, 6, 18, 20
nonstandard tool 10
number line 4, 15
reasonable 10, 14
subtract 16
total 16, 18, 20, 21
zero 6, 18